ANTI-GRAVITY
CAKES

ANTI-GRAVITY CAKES

25 bakes that defy belief

JAYNE CROSS

LORENZ BOOKS

CONTENTS

INTRODUCTION

Cakes that tumble, soar and even fly – here are edible constructions that seemingly defy gravity and that are guaranteed to get reactions of amazement and amusement. The creative possiblities of cakes that you can make on an anti-gravity theme are vast, and within this book I have created a selection to cover all kinds of occasions as well as catering for a range of different skill levels. From a very simple buttercream-covered giant cupcake topped with sprinkles, through to precariously balanced building blocks for a toddler, or an intriguing suspended watering can that is perpetually sprinkling a flowerpot, there should be something just right to add the finishing flourish to your special event.

Each recipe has full step-by-step instructions; if you are new to some elements of sugarpaste work they are easy to follow and will introduce you to some skills. Cake decorating takes patience and planning ahead to allow icing and other elements to set in order to achieve the best results, so read each recipe carefully before you start to ensure you have allowed enough time. Many of the decorations can be made several days in advance, as can the sponge cakes, so that all the elements will be ready for when you come to assemble the cake.

Although some of the cakes in the book can be made without specialist anti-gravity equipment most of them do call for it and so it is worth investing in a kit. These kits include base boards and foundation rods which are essential for anchoring cakes to the boards and so allowing the anti-gravity element to balance securely.

Once you've mastered these designs, experiment with your own, adapting skills learnt from this book. I find a lot of inspiration from day-to-day objects – colours and flowers from cards, pictures and postcards, or from jars of sweets or candies stacked in a shop. The person you are making the cake for may also inspire an idea or theme to make it really personal. Once you've used the anti-gravity kits a few times you will discover many more ways that they can be used to create different shapes and combinations. I hope that you enjoy the cake projects in this book and that they will inspire you to go on and develop lovely designs of your own.

EQUIPMENT

The fantastical nature of the cakes rely, as with most magical illusions, on some behind-the-scenes tricks of the trade. The secret elements are not out of reach however and a simple speciality kit will provide the majority of what you need.

There is now a range of shapes and sizes of cake novelty construction kits available; we've used standard items that are usually interchangeable or adaptable. Otherwise you'll just need a basic range of kitchen equipment.

Most structures need the support of rods which are secured in base boards. The foundation rods are held in place by locking nuts and then extra rods are inserted into these rods to support the cakes as well as providing a firm base for you to insert further rods, wires or dowels, which are used to carry the anti-gravity element of each cake. For designs where the piece that you are balancing is light, however, you can use wooden dowels or skewers pushed into the cake and sit the cake directly on to a covered cake drum, or on a cake stand or plate.

Base boards: round or square and in different sizes, these have holes which are used for the supporting rods. The projects in this book use five-hole boards, typically 25cm/10in.

Platforms: round or square and in different sizes, typically 15cm/6in and 10cm/4in, these are thinner than a base board and are used to suspend part of the structure. The projects in this book use five-hole platforms.

Blanking caps: these are used to cover the holes not in use.

Foundation rods: these are long or short and lock into the base boards, secured with a locking nut on the underside. Standard lengths are long (12cm/4½in) and short (3cm/1⅛in).

Rods: short, medium and long, these are used to extend the structure to the required length. Standard lengths are long (10cm/4in), medium (5cm/2in) and short (2.5cm/1in).

Joints: the elbow joint is curved, allowing you to redirect the angle of the rods or structure; the single- or double-angled joints allow branches to be created in the structure. Connectors, collars and adaptors are sometimes used, and are part of most anti-gravity cake kits.

Dowels: these provide firm thin lengths, usually supported in the cake within a hollow rod or pushed directly into the cake, and any exposed length can be disguised with icing or decorative elements. They are available in plastic or wood, and both can be used although wooden ones are easier to cut to length.

Wire: this is used to create thin shaped extensions to the structures, and can be covered with icing to disguise them. Choose a thickness that is strong but pliable. This is best sourced from a hardware store as florist's wire is usually not strong enough. Be sure to clean before use.

Florist's wire: this thin wire comes in white, silver and green and various thicknesses. It is ideal to use for small 'splashes' or 'sparks' as it can be easily shaped and covered in candy melts to hide it. This wire is measured by gauge and the best gauge to use is 22.

CAKE SAFETY

Some of the elements used to create these cakes aren't edible, such as the wires and wooden dowels, and while it might be tempting to small children to try to eat the icing or candy melts covering these pieces it should be avoided as the ends of the wire might be sharp and small splinters might come off the wooden dowels. So when you come to serve the cakes these items are best removed and put out of temptation's way. There are plenty of other lovely edible parts to each of the cakes that can be enjoyed.

To serve the layered cakes it is best to separate the layers first and then cut into slices; you don't need to remove any rods in the centres of the cakes, just cut up to and around them.

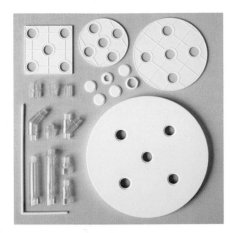

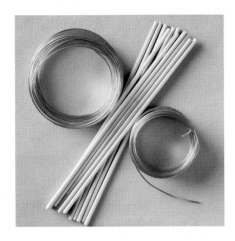

Above: Specalist cake construction kits typically offer round and square cake platforms in a range of sizes, and larger base boards. These might have five or nine holes, in which foundation rods are secured with locking nuts or 'sealed' with blanking caps. The rods, connectors and adaptors come in a range of lengths and angles.

Above: Cake decorating equipment you will find useful for perfecting the appearance of the cake include (from left) a ruler for measuring and making straight lines, spacers, edible glue, brushes, a range of modelling tools, tweezers, a piping bag, palette knives, icing smoothers and a spirit level.

Above: Dowels and wire are thin but strong, and form a useful invisible part of the construction in some anti-gravity cake designs. The flexibility of wire allows all kinds of impossible-seeming shapes to be created.

Cake boards: some recipes use regular drum-style cake boards rather than the specific anti-gravity base boards, as foundation rods are not needed in the construction.

Cake tins or pans: round and square tins come in a variety of sizes. Nearly all of the cakes in the book use deep cake tins – I recommend buying the best quality that you can afford as they tend to be heavier and will cook your cakes more evenly.

Bowls: in a variety of sizes for mixing cake batter and icing.

Cooling racks: made from wire, these allow the air to pass round the cakes so they cool completely without becoming soggy.

Sieve or strainer: this is essential to sift flour and icing sugar to give a lighter cake mix and ensure smooth icing and buttercream.

Rolling pins: both large and small, for rolling out pastes.

Ruler: an essential piece of equipment for cake decorating.

Spirit level: useful for checking that your cake is level before covering it in sugarpaste.

Shaping tools: a wide variety is available, to make shaping sugarpaste easier and give a more professional finish.

Cookie cutters: available in a large range of shapes and sizes and used for cutting sugarpaste or flower paste shapes.

Cake lifter: a large flat disc which, although not essential, is very useful for lifting cakes on to cake boards easily without damaging the sugarpaste.

Smoothers: for giving a smooth, even finish to covered cakes.

Spacers: useful guides for rolling out sugarpaste evenly.

Palette knives: it is good to have a range of sizes for applying butter-cream and other icings as well as for lifting decorations on to cakes.

Piping or pastry bags: both large and small for piping with royal icing or buttercream.

Piping nozzles: available in a large variety of sizes, both metal and plastic, and these are either plain or star shaped. There are also more specialist shaped nozzles which can be used to pipe other decorations.

Cocktail sticks or toothpicks: useful for adding food colouring to icing and also for marking cakes when shaping or levelling.

Edible glue: essential for sticking sugarpaste together as well as for attaching ribbon to cake boards.

Florist's tape: available in many colours and used to cover wire.

Flower cutters: available in many shapes and sizes and as simple metal cutters or plunger cutters.

Foam pad: used for shaping flower petals and other shapes as they dry.

Paintbrushes: useful to have a range of sizes for decorating cakes as well as applying glue.

Tweezers: handy for lifting tiny pieces of sugarpaste or flower paste into place.

Madeira Cake

Madeira cake is a firm, moist cake that is ideal for anti-gravity constructions. It carves and shapes well and is very suitable for covering in sugarpaste. It will keep for up to two weeks which is useful when you need to assemble the cake project over a few days.

1 First preheat the oven to 160°C/ 325°F/Gas 3. Grease and line the cake tin or pan with baking parchment and set to one side.

2 Put the softened butter and caster sugar in the bowl of a free-standing mixer or a large mixing bowl and beat until pale and creamy. Lightly beat the eggs together then add a little at a time to the creamed mixture, beating well between each addition.

3 Sift the flours together into the bowl and gently fold into the mixture, making sure that the flour is fully incorporated.

4 Spoon the mixture into the prepared tin, smooth the top with the back of a spoon and bake in the oven for the time according to the table below, or until the cake is golden brown, well risen and a skewer inserted into the centre of the cake comes out clean. If the top of the cake starts to brown too much during cooking, then gently lay a piece of baking parchment over the tin to protect it for the final cooking time.

5 Leave the cake to cool in the tin for 15 minutes then turn out from the tin on to a wire rack and leave to cool completely. If you are not going to use the cake straight away, then wrap in some baking parchment and keep in an airtight container until needed.

6 If the cake has risen unevenly, it can be trimmed flat with a large serrated knife, see box right.

> Choose a square or round cake tin according to the project. Most of the cakes in this book require a deep rather than a shallow tin, which is what the chart below assumes.

Cake tin/pan sizes	12.5cm/5in round 10cm/4in square	15cm/6in round 12.5cm/5in square	18cm/7in round 15cm/6in square	20cm/8in round 18cm/7in square	23cm/9in round 20cm/8in square	25cm/10in round 23cm/9in square	28cm/11in round 25cm/10in square
Unsalted butter	115g/4oz	175g/6oz	225g/8oz	350g/12oz	450g/1lb	500g/1¼lb	700g/1lb 9oz
Caster (superfine) sugar	115g/4oz	175g/6oz	225g/8oz	350g/12oz	450g/1lb	500g/1¼lb	700g/1lb 9oz
Self-raising (self-rising) flour	115g/4oz	175g/6oz	225g/8oz	350g/12oz	450g/1lb	500g/1¼lb	700g/1lb 9oz
Plain (all-purpose) flour	50g/2oz	75g/3oz	100g/3½oz	150g/5oz	200g/7oz	225g/8oz	300g/11oz
Medium (US large) eggs	2	3	4	6	8	9	12
Baking times	45mins–1 hour	1–1¼ hours	1–1¼ hours	1¼–1½ hours	1½–1¾ hours	1½–1¾ hours	1¾–2 hours

HOW TO LEVEL CAKES

Place the baked cake on a large board. Use a ruler to mark around the top edge of the cake at an even height all the way round (you can use cocktail sticks or toothpicks to mark the height). When you have measured all the way round use a large serrated knife to cut the top off the cake. To check if the cake is level you could use a spirit level – place it in the centre of the cake and trim again if the cake is still uneven.

Chocolate Cake

A chocolate-flavoured madeira has cocoa for colour and interest but retains the same firm but moist texture as the plain cake, with the keeping qualities and the density needed for covering in sugarpaste and decorations.

1 First preheat the oven to 160°C/ 325°F/Gas 3. Grease and line the cake tin or pan with baking parchment and set to one side.

2 Put the softened butter and caster sugar in a large mixing bowl or the bowl of a free-standing mixer and beat until pale and creamy. Lightly beat the eggs together then add a little at a time to the creamed mixture, beating well between each addition.

3 Sift the flours and cocoa powder together into the bowl and gently fold into the mixture, making sure

you scrape right down to the bottom of the bowl to ensure that the flour is fully incorporated.

4 Spoon the mixture into the prepared tin, smooth the top with the back of a spoon and bake in the oven for the time according to the table below, or until the cake is browned, well risen and a skewer inserted into the centre of the cake comes out clean. If the top of the cake starts to brown too much during cooking, then gently lay a piece of baking parchment over the tin to protect it for the final cooking time.

5 Leave the cake to cool in the tin for 15 minutes then turn out and leave to cool completely on a wire rack. If you are not going to use the cake straight away, wrap in some baking parchment and keep in an airtight container until needed. Level the cake before using.

When storing you want the cake to retain its moisture so use an airtight container but make sure the sponge is completely cold, otherwise condensation will form.

Cake tin/pan sizes	12.5cm/5in round 10cm/4in square	15cm/6in round 12.5cm/5in square	18cm/7in round 15cm/6in square	20cm/8in round 18cm/7in square	23cm/9in round 20cm/8in square	25cm/10in round 23cm/9in square	28cm/11in round 25cm/10in square
Unsalted butter	115g/4oz	175g/6oz	225g/8oz	350g/12oz	450g/1lb	500g/1¼lb	700g/1lb 9oz
Caster (superfine sugar	115g/4oz	175g/6oz	225g/8oz	350g/12oz	450g/1lb	500g/1¼lb	700g/1lb 9oz
Self-raising (self-rising) flour	115g/4oz	175g/6oz	225g/8oz	350g/12oz	450g/1lb	500g1¼lb	700g/1lb 9oz
Plain flour (all-purpose)	25g/1oz	50g/2oz	50g/2oz	75g/3oz	125g/4oz	125g/4oz	175g/6oz
Cocoa	25g/1oz	25g/1oz	50g/2oz	75g/3oz	75g/3oz	100g/3½oz	125g/4oz
Medium (US large) eggs	2	3	4	6	8	9	12
Baking times	45mins–1 hour	1–1¼ hours	1–1¼ hours	1–1¼-1½ hours	1½–1¾ hours	1½–1¾ hours	1¾–2 hours

HOW TO LINE A CAKE TIN OR PAN

Put the tin on a sheet of baking parchment, draw around the outside edge and cut out the shape. Cut a strip that is long enough to cover around the sides of the tin. Make a fold along a long edge of the strip about 2cm/¾in deep, and snip all along the folded edge to the crease at about 1cm/½in intervals. Grease the inside of the tin then press the strip of baking parchment inside the tin with the crease against the bottom edge so that the snipped edge sits on the bottom of the tin. Put the cut shape on top of the snipped edge on the base of the tin and smooth down.

Sugarpaste

Sugarpaste is used to cover most of the cakes and cake boards in this book. It is readily available in most supermarkets as well as specialist cake suppliers in a great variety of colours. However it is also straightforward to make your own.

1 egg white
30ml/2 tbsp liquid glucose
500g/1¼lb icing (confectioners') sugar,
plus extra for dusting and kneading

1 Put the egg white and liquid glucose in a large, clean bowl. Beat together lightly.

2 Sift the icing sugar into the bowl and stir together with a wooden spoon until the mixture starts to bind together, then work with your hand until a firm paste forms.

3 Turn the sugarpaste out on to a work surface lightly dusted with icing sugar and bring together into a ball. Knead it lightly; if it is too sticky add a little more icing sugar until it is firm and pliable. Knead the sugarpaste with the heels of your hands until it is smooth and no cracks appear as you work.

4 Wrap the sugarpaste in clear film or plastic wrap and then store in a plastic bag until ready to use for rolling and covering cakes and boards – detailed instructions follow overleaf. Sugarpaste will keep for 2–3 weeks.

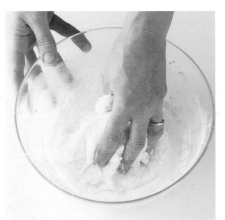

CANDY MELTS

These are very versatile cake decorating ingredients, available in a huge range of colours. Made of sugar, milk solids and vegetable oils, they are melted and used in this book for joining, covering up unsightly elements and for piping.

To melt, put into a microwave-safe container and heat for about 1 minute, on medium power, stir thoroughly, and microwave again if necessary. They can also be melted in a bowl set over a pan of gently simmering water, stirring all the time.

FLOWER PASTE

Flower paste sets harder than sugarpaste and so is used to make flowers and other decorations. It is available from cake decorating suppliers in a wide variety of colours, but it is very easy to make your own.

**250g/9oz sugarpaste, of any colour
5ml/1 tsp gum tragacanth**

1 Make a well in the centre of the sugarpaste and add the gum tragacanth. Fold the edges of the sugarpaste over the centre and knead well to ensure the gum tragacanth is fully incorporated.

2 Wrap the flower paste in clear film or plastic wrap and place in a plastic bag. Leave to rest for at least an hour before using, ideally leaving overnight.

HOW TO COLOUR SUGARPASTE

There are many colours of sugarpaste ready to buy but it is easy to colour your own, either by adding colouring paste to sugarpaste or by mixing different colours of sugarpaste together. It is best to use a paste form of food colouring rather than liquid as it is more concentrated and also won't affect the texture as much. Use the tip of a cocktail stick or toothpick and add a little food colouring to the white sugarpaste. Knead well to ensure the colouring is fully mixed in before adding any more. The colour will deepen slightly as the sugarpaste rests so add the food colouring gradually.

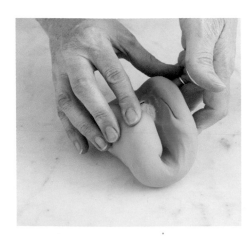

Building Block Tower

These fun playtime blocks are a great birthday cake for younger children. The colours of the icing can easily be changed, as can the motifs on the sides, to truly personalise it. The blocks are best iced the day before assembling.

FOR THE CAKE

25cm/10in square madeira cake (see page 10)

⅓ quantity buttercream (see page 14)

750g/1lb 10oz red sugarpaste

750g/1lb 10oz yellow sugarpaste

750g/1lb 10oz blue sugarpaste

500g/1¼lb white sugarpaste

Edible glue

15ml/1 tbsp royal icing

50g/2oz green sugarpaste

50g/2oz brown sugarpaste

EQUIPMENT

2 x 10cm/4in square platforms

Sharp knife

Rolling pin

Baking parchment

11 blanking caps

30cm/12in square base board

2 long foundation rods

2 locking nuts

Narrow red ribbon

Apple corer

2 collars

3 x 10cm/4in long rods

2.5cm/1in short rod

2 elbow joints

Number cutters

Shape cutters

Teddy bear cutter

METHOD

1 To make the blocks, cut the cake in half then half again, using a cake platform as a guide to create 4 x 10cm/4in blocks. Cut one into 3 horizontally so that you have 3 thin slices 2.5cm/1in x 10cm/4in. Add 1 of these slices to each of the other 3 blocks so that you now have 3 x 10cm/4in cubes. Stick together with a little buttercream, trimming the edges again if necessary to ensure the edges are as straight as possible.

2 Cover one of the cubes on all sides with a layer of buttercream. Roll out the red sugarpaste and cut out 6 x 10cm/4in square pieces; you may need to re-roll to get the last 2 squares out of the piece. Place one square on to one side of the cake and gently smooth, then repeat with the other 5 squares so that the cake is covered completely. Smooth all the sides and edges to get the cube as even as possible. Set aside on baking parchment. Repeat with the remaining 2 cake cubes covering one in the yellow sugarpaste and one in blue, keeping the trimmings for the decorations. Leave overnight to dry.

3 Fit the blanking caps into 3 of the outer holes of the base board. Cover it with the white sugarpaste (see page 19) and make a hole in the centre of the board and the remaining outer hole for the foundation rods.

Champagne Cake

A champagne glass overflowing with bubbles makes this a fun but sophisticated cake for a celebration. Only basic modelling skills are required although good balancing skills are needed for the assembly! A plastic bottle is lighter if you can find one.

FOR THE CAKE

400g/14oz ivory sugarpaste
Edible glue
250g/9oz ivory flower paste
20cm/8in round madeira
   cake (see page 10)
¼ quantity buttercream (see
   page 14)
1kg/2¼lb black sugarpaste
25g/1oz royal icing
Gold shimmer pearls
Ivory shimmer pearls
Gold edible glitter
Gold edible confetti

EQUIPMENT

4 blanking caps
25cm/10in round base
   board
Short foundation rod
Locking nut
Short rod
Connector
2 narrow gold ribbons
Rolling pin
Ruler
13cm/5in round cutter
7cm/2¾in round cutter
Martini glass
2.5cm/1in round cutter
10cm/4in long rod
Metal skewer
Apple corer
Sharp knife
60cm/24in piece of wire
Wide gold organza ribbon
Pins (optional)
Small (empty) champagne
   bottle

METHOD

1 Fit the blanking caps into the 4 outer holes of the base board. Cover the board with the ivory sugarpaste (see page 19) and make a hole in the centre of the board for the foundation rod. Attach the rod to the board with the locking nut, then add the short rod and connector and leave to set overnight. Using a little edible glue stick one of the narrow gold ribbons around the board.

2 To make the champagne glass roll out the ivory flower paste and cut out a 13cm/5in circle and a 7cm/2¾in circle. Cut a quarter wedge out of the larger circle then brush one of the straight cut edges with a little edible glue. Seal the two straight edges then place inside the martini glass and gently smooth down to create the shape of the glass and smooth the top edge. Cut a 2.5cm/1in hole from the centre of the smaller circle. This will be the foot of the glass.

3 Reroll the rest of the flower paste into a rectangle 9cm/3½in x 7cm/

2¾in. Brush the long rod with a little edible glue then wrap the rectangle around the long rod, trimming away any excess where the long edges meet. Gently roll the rod to smooth the surface. Trim the ends and smooth the edges. Leave these pieces to harden slightly for a couple of hours before removing the glass.

4 To make the icing glass, stand the rod upright and using a little edible glue stick the bowl shape to the top. Push the top edge of the rod up through the base of the bowl and press gently together to secure and smooth the join. Using a metal skewer, make a hole in the base of the glass for the wire to go through the rod or 'stem'. Leave to dry again overnight or for at least 24 hours.

5 When ready to assemble, make a hole in the centre of the cake with an apple corer for the rod. Ensure the hole goes right through the cake and rub the hole lightly with your finger to remove excess crumbs.

6 Cover the top, bottom and sides of the lid cake with buttercream. Fit the remaining 4 blanking caps to the outer holes of the platform and attach the short foundation rod to the centre hole, with the locking nut.

7 Place the platform against the lid cake with the locking nut against the sponge. Then spread more buttercream over the exposed side of the platform.

8 Roll out the remaining purple sugarpaste and cut out 2 x 13cm/5in circles and a strip 3cm/1⅛in x 40cm/15¾in. Cut a 2cm/¾in hole in one of the circles and then cover the base of the lid with that, placing the hole over the short foundation rod. Cover the top of the lid with the other whole circle of sugarpaste. Dampen the edges of both circles with a little cooled boiled water and attach the strip of sugarpaste around the edge of the lid, over the buttercream sides, smoothing as you go.

9 Attach the single angle joint to the long foundation rod and then add the long rod to the joint. Attach the lid to the long rod.

10 Fill the box with the chocolates, piling them high so that you cover the rods. Attach the bow to the top of the lid. Attach the narrow gold ribbon around the edge of the lid and attach the wide gold ribbon around the middle of the main cake using edible glue, and if need be pins to secure the ribbons at the back. Finally attach the narrow purple ribbon to the centre of the wide gold ribbon.

5 To make the holly leaves and berries, roll out the dark green flower paste and cut out 3 holly leaves, curve slightly and set aside. Roll 3 small balls from a little of the remaining red flower paste for the berries and leave both overnight to dry.

6 Fit the blanking caps into the 4 outer holes of the base board. Cover the board with the red sugarpaste (see page 19) and make a hole in the centre of the board for the long foundation rod.

7 Attach the rod to the board with the locking nut and leave to set overnight. Using a little glue stick the narrow gold ribbon around the edge of the board.

8 When ready to assemble, using an apple corer make a hole in the centre of the Christmas pudding for the rod to fit through, ensuring the hole goes right through the pudding. Lift the pudding on to the covered board over the foundation rod then attach the elbow joint and the long rod to the foundation rod.

9 Gently melt the candy melts either on a medium heat in the microwave or over a pan of gently simmering water; be careful not to overheat or it will turn grainy. Use a little of the candy melts to stick the wooden dowel

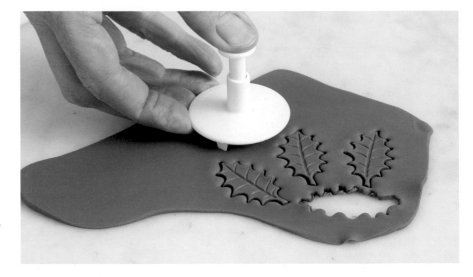

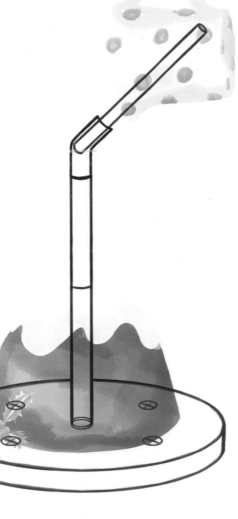

into the jug at an angle so that it comes out of the lip at a downward slope, and leave to set.

10 Put the rest of the candy melts into the piping bag and snip off the tip. Pipe the candy melts on to the rods and elbow joint, ensuring they are covered entirely, then pipe the rest on to the top of the Christmas pudding and down the sides slightly.

11 Insert the wooden dowel into the end of the elbow joint and add a little more of the candy melts to secure.

12 Place the holly leaves and berries on the board at the base of the pudding. Leave to set for 30 minutes before serving. Don't pour brandy over this pudding to set alight!

Posy of Daisies

A cheerful floral tree growing in a presentation garden pot – this offers flowers and cake in one! The delicate daisies need to be made in advance to ensure they hold their shape. You could of course make different styles and colours of flowers.

FOR THE CAKE

250g/9oz white flower paste
50g/2oz yellow flower paste
Edible glue
800g/1¾lb yellow
   sugarpaste
15cm/6in round madeira
   cake (see page 10)
12.5cm/5in round madeira
   cake (see page 10)
¼ quantity buttercream (see
   page 14)
500g/1¼lb navy blue
   sugarpaste
50g/2oz royal icing
Green sugar crystals
Green shimmer pearls

EQUIPMENT

Rolling pin
Large daisy cutter
Foam pad
Shaping tool
Flower formers
Sieve or strainer
12cm/4½in diameter
   polystyrene or
   Styrofoam ball
Metal skewer
Wooden dowel
Green florist's tape
Polystyrene cake dummy
   (or spare base board with
   long rod)
4 blanking caps
25cm/10in round base
   board
Long foundation rod
Locking nut
Narrow yellow ribbon
Ruler
Spare wooden dowel
Large serrated knife
Pastry brush
Apple corer
Embossing rolling pin
Green ribbon

METHOD

1 To make the daisies, roll out the white flower paste as thinly as possible and cut out flowers with a daisy cutter. Place a flower on to your foam pad and with a shaping tool gently roll each petal to thin slightly, then transfer the daisy to a flower former to dry. You'll need about 36 daisies in total.

2 Once you've shaped all the daisies make the centres. Take the yellow flower paste and divide into 36 pieces. Roll each piece into a small ball and press one side of the ball on to the outside of the sieve or strainer flattening the ball slightly as you press to create a pattern on the paste. Dab a little edible glue in the middle of each daisy and stick in a yellow centre. Leave for at least 24 hours to dry.

3 Make a hole in the polystyrene ball about 5cm/2in deep with a metal skewer. Push the dowel into the hole to make sure it fits, then take out and cover with the green florist's tape. Add some glue to the dowel and then push it back into the ball. Put the other end into a cake dummy or a long rod fitted into a spare cake board, and leave to dry for about 30 minutes.

4 In the meantime, fit the blanking caps into the 4 outer holes of the 25cm/10in round base board. Cover the board with 400g/14oz of the yellow sugarpaste (see page 19) and make a hole in the middle for the long foundation rod. Attach the rod to the board with the locking nut and leave to set overnight. Using a little glue stick the narrow yellow ribbon around the edge of the board.

5 Roll out the remaining yellow sugarpaste to a 45cm/18in circle. Brush the ball with a little cooled boiled water and drape the sugarpaste over, gently moulding to fit as neatly as possible and trimming away any excess. Leave to set overnight.

6 When ready to assemble, place the larger cake on top of the smaller one, push a spare wooden dowel through the centre of the cakes to hold them in place, then with a large serrated knife trim the sides of both cakes to form a flowerpot shape. Brush away any excess crumbs with a pastry brush, then make a larger hole in the centre with an apple corer, making sure the hole goes right through both cakes.

7 Sandwich the cakes together with a little of the buttercream and then cover the top and sides with the remaining buttercream. Roll out the navy sugarpaste and cut to a rectangle 45cm/18in x 15cm/6in, then using the embossing rolling pin create a pattern over the surface of the icing. Use this to cover the sides of the flowerpot.

8 Roll out a strip of navy blue sugarpaste 2.5cm/1in x 45cm/18in. Brush a little cooled boiled water to

the top edge of the pot and stick the strip to this, pressing down gently to seal. Make sure the edge of the strip stands slightly proud from the top surface of the cake to allow room for the sugar crystals.

9 Gently lift the cake on to the covered board over the foundation rod and smooth the sides of the cake to ensure the icing neatly meets the icing on the board – be very careful that you don't smooth too much or you will lose the pattern.

10 Insert the covered ball into the foundation rod then, adding a dab of royal icing to the back of each daisy, stick them to the ball until the whole ball is covered. Tie the green ribbon around the dowel and add the sugar crystals and shimmer pearls to the pot.

Easter Egg Nest

Multi-coloured mini eggs tumbling into a chocolate nest. Using all ready-made ingredients, this cake is deceptively easy to make and assemble, and is a chocoholic's dream come true, perfect for Easter tea.

FOR THE CAKE

400g/14oz duck egg blue
sugarpaste
Edible glue
23cm/9in round chocolate
cake (see page 12)
⅓ quantity chocolate
buttercream (see page 14)
4 packs chocolate finger
biscuits or cookies
50g/2oz brown candy melts
4 packets chocolate mini
eggs
1 large chocolate Easter egg

EQUIPMENT

4 blanking caps
25cm/10in round base
board
Long foundation rod
Locking nut
Narrow duck egg blue
ribbon
Small serrated knife
Apple corer
Pastry brush
10cm/4in long rod
Elbow joint
Connector
Single angled joint
Small palette knife
Small sharp knife

METHOD

1 Fit the blanking caps into the 4 outer holes of the base board. Cover the board with the duck egg blue sugarpaste (see page 19) and make a hole in the centre of the board for the foundation rod. Attach the rod to the board with the locking nut and leave to set overnight. Using a little glue stick the narrow duck egg blue ribbon around the edge of the board.

2 When ready to assemble, shape the cake with a small serrated knife to create a nest shape, then hollow out the middle for the eggs to sit in. Using the apple corer cut a hole in the centre of the cake for the foundation rod to go through. Brush away the excess crumbs from the cake with a pastry brush.

7 In a small bowl melt the candy melts, either in the microwave on a medium heat, or over a pan of gently simmering water. Using a small palette knife coat the whole of the rods and joints with the candy melts.

8 Starting at the bottom of the rods stick the mini eggs by adding a little extra melted candy melts to each egg and holding it in place for a few seconds to make sure that they stick firmly. Ensure that the entire rod is covered and, if needed, add extra eggs on top of the first layer. Place the remaining eggs in the base of the nest.

3 Cover the outside of the cake with the chocolate buttercream in a thick even layer, ensuring all of the cake is covered.

4 Gently lift the cake on to the cake board over the foundation rod. Then use the chocolate fingers to cover the outside edges of the cake – use a combination of whole and broken biscuits and make sure there are no gaps. You may need to add a dab of buttercream to each biscuit to help them stick.

5 Spread the remaining buttercream on the inside of the cake and use the remaining biscuits to cover that in the same way.

6 Attach the long rod, elbow joint, connector and finally the single angled joint to the foundation rod in the centre of the cake.

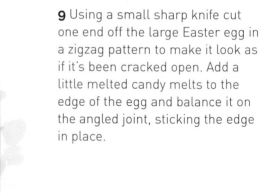

9 Using a small sharp knife cut one end off the large Easter egg in a zigzag pattern to make it look as if it's been cracked open. Add a little melted candy melts to the edge of the egg and balance it on the angled joint, sticking the edge in place.

A Miniature Garden

A potted garden of roses being permanently watered, this is one for the gardener in your life. The watering can and roses need making the day before and are perhaps for the more experienced decorator. One of the silicone moulds will have a hole cut out of it, so can't be re-used.

FOR THE CAKES

400g/14oz green sugarpaste

Edible glue

250g/9oz pale grey flower paste

75g/3oz red flower paste

75g/3oz pink flower paste

75g/3oz pale pink flower paste

50g/2oz pale green flower paste

Cake mix for 13cm/5in chocolate cake (see page 12)

100g/3½oz Oreo cookies or other chocolate biscuits

¼ quantity chocolate buttercream (see page 14)

100g/3½oz blue candy melts

EQUIPMENT

4 blanking caps

25cm/10in round base board

Long foundation rod

Locking nut

Narrow green ribbon

Rolling pin

Sharp knife

6cm/2½in round cutter

Ruler

Paper

Wooden dowel

Small leaf cutter

Chopstick

9 silicone flowerpot muffin moulds

12-hole muffin tin or pan

Skewer

Apple corer

Food processor

Elbow joint

5mm/¼in plain nozzle

Small piping (pastry) bag

22-gauge wire

METHOD

1 Fit the blanking caps into the 4 outer holes of the base board. Cover the board with the green sugarpaste (see page 19) and make a hole in the centre of the board for the foundation rod. Attach the rod to the board with the locking nut and leave to set overnight. Using a little edible glue, stick the narrow green ribbon around the edge of the board.

2 Meanwhile, to make the watering can, roll out the pale grey flower paste and cut out a 6cm/2½in circle and a rectangle 6cm/2½in x 20cm/8in. Dampen the edge of the circle with a little glue and then wrap one edge of the rectangle around the outside, sticking the edges together to seal. Leave to dry for a couple of hours to set a little.

3 Roll out a little more of the remaining pale grey flower paste and cut 2 thin strips 5mm/¼in x 20cm/8in. Brush the back of each strip with a little glue and stick each one around the body of the watering can, one near the top and one near the base, pressing lightly to secure.

4 Cut out another pale grey 6cm/2½in circle and using the same round cutter stamp out one side of the circle. Brush the top edge of the watering can and attach this part-circle to the top, raising the centre a little to shape it.

5 Roll out about half of the remaining grey flower paste and cut 2 strips for the handles, one 8cm/3⅛in x 7.5mm/⅓in and one 1cm/½in x 6cm/2½in. Glue the longer handle to the top of the watering can and using a little roll of paper to support the handle as it dries. Take the shorter length and attach to the side of the can to create the handle shape.

6 Cut the wooden dowel to 20cm/8in and insert one end into the watering can at an angle – this is to support the spout. Roll the remaining flower paste into a sausage shape 4cm/1½in long, cut the base at an angle and brush this with a little glue. Push this over the wooden dowel and reshape to ensure it covers the dowel evenly and sticks to the side of the watering can.

7 Take the trimmings from this sausage and shape into a cone shape, flatten the end then push this over the end of the dowel to create the end of the spout.

8 To make the roses roll out the red flower paste into a rectangle and cut strips 1.2cm/⅔in x 10cm/4in. Gently roll up each strip to form the roses, shaping them as you roll. Pinch the bottom edge together to seal. You need 9 roses. Repeat with both the pink and pale pink flower paste so that you have 27 roses in total. Roll out the pale green flower paste and cut out 27 small leaves; add a curve to some of the leaves by draping them over a chopstick as they dry. Leave the watering can, roses and leaves to dry for at least 24 hours.

9 Cut a hole in the centre of the base of one of the silicone moulds

for the foundation rod to fit through then grease all the flowerpot moulds and place into the holes in the muffin tin. Preheat the oven to 190°C/375°F/Gas 5.

10 Make the cake mix (see page 12) and divide between the muffin moulds. Bake for 15–18 minutes until firm to the touch and when a skewer inserted in the centre comes out clean. Set aside to cool.

11 When ready to assemble, using an apple corer make a hole in the centre of the cake with the hole in the base, for the rod to fit through. Place this on the covered cake board over the rod.

12 Blitz the Oreo cookies in a food processor to create crumbs for the soil. Spread the top of each cake with a thick layer of buttercream and the Oreo crumbs.

13 Insert the elbow joint into the rod then put the watering can in place by inserting the end of the wooden dowel into the joint.

14 Gently melt the candy melts either on a medium heat in the microwave or over a pan of gently simmering water; be careful not to overheat or it will turn grainy. Fit the nozzle in the piping bag and fill with the melted candy melts. Pipe on to the rod starting at the spout of the watering can, working down to the Oreo crumbs to create the flow of water and ensuring the whole of the rod is covered.

15 Cut short lengths of the wire then dip one end into the candy melt and pipe a blob on the ends to create a splash of water. Leave to dry then add them to the flowerpot. Finally, arrange the roses and leaves on the flowerpots.

Flying a Kite

The topsy-turvy layering of this hilly cake creates a delightful winding path to the top. Simple flowers and toadstools provide visual and edible treats along the way. All the decorations need to be made the day before assembly.

FOR THE CAKES

2kg/4½lb green sugarpaste
Edible glue
50g/2oz yellow flower paste
50g/2oz red flower paste
25g/1oz navy blue flower paste
50g/2oz royal icing
25g/1oz orange flower paste
25g/1oz purple flower paste
25g/1oz pale yellow flower paste
25g/1oz white flower paste
20cm/8in round madeira cake (see page 10)
15cm/6in round madeira cake (see page 10)
½ quantity buttercream (see page 14)

EQUIPMENT

Rolling pin
25cm/10in round cake board
Narrow green ribbon
Sharp knife
Ruler
45cm/18in wire
White florist's tape
Small daisy cutter
Medium daisy cutter
Small flower blossom plunger cutter
Medium flower blossom plunger cutter
Foam pad
2 small piping (pastry) bags
No. 2 plain nozzle
Spirit level (optional)
Small sieve or strainer
Small rabbit figure for the top of the cake (optional)

METHOD

1 Roll out 400g/14oz of the green sugarpaste and use this to cover the cake board (see page 19). Leave to dry overnight and using a little glue, stick the ribbon around the edge.

2 To make the kite, roll out the yellow flower paste and cut out 2 small triangles and 2 large triangles (using the template on page 125). Repeat with the red flower paste. Using edible glue stick the kite pieces together so that you have 2 kite shapes. From yellow, red and blue flower paste cut out small bows for the kite string. Make 2 small indents in the middle of each bow to look like the knot.

3 To make the string, cover the wire with a length of white florist's tape, wrapping it tightly around the wire. Place one end of the wire down the centre of one of the kite pieces, and using royal icing as glue, stick on the second kite piece. Gently press the two pieces together and smooth the edges and wipe away any excess royal icing.

4 To make the flowers, roll out the different colours of flower paste and cut out shapes. Roll tiny balls for the centres. Use plunger cutters for the blossom flowers and push out on to a foam pad so they curve up at the edges.

5 To make the toadstools roll the white flower paste into a long sausage about 5mm/¼in in diameter then cut into short lengths between 1–1.5cm/½–⅔in long. Take the remaining red flower paste and roll into small balls to form the tops of the toadstools. Cut each ball in half then attach these halves to the white pieces of flower paste with a little edible glue, sticking them flat side down. Pipe small dots on top of each toadstool with the royal icing.

6 Then using the remaining royal icing, pipe a little icing on to the back of each bow and then stick them down the kite string alternating colours and spacing them out. Leave the kite, flowers and toadstools to dry overnight.

7 When ready to assemble, take the larger cake and cut the top off at a 45° angle starting from the top of the cake on one side and cutting down to leave a depth of 4cm/1½in on the other side. Trim the top section that you have cut off so that it forms a circle 17.5cm/7¾in in diameter and then trim the top so that it is flat.

8 Place the cut piece back on top of the 20cm/8in base matching the back edges and placing the thicker side of the cut piece on top of the thinner side of the base cake so that the top of this cake is level. You might need to play around with exactly where it sits to make sure it is flat, use a spirit level to check this, but make sure that you have space in front of and to each side of the top cake as this will form the path up the hill.

9 Once you are happy the positioning, use a little of the buttercream to stick the two pieces together. Then with 1kg/2¼lb of the green sugarpaste and two-thirds of the buttercream cover this doubled cake (page 19). Cover the smaller cake with buttercream and 500g/1¼lb green sugarpaste.

10 Apply a blob of buttercream to the centre of the covered cake board and gently lift the larger cake on to the board, positioning it towards the back of the board to allow room for the flowers and grass at the front.

11 Add another blob of buttercream to the top of the larger cake and gently lift the smaller cake on top with the back edges of the cakes matching up to make the path at the front and sides. Smooth the icing down on the smaller cake so that it neatly meets the icing on the cake below.

12 Take the kite and push the wire into the centre of the top cake pushing it right through all the layers so that it is stable.

13 To make the grass, take a ball of green sugarpaste and push it through a sieve or strainer to create blades of grass. Put the sieve flat side down and use a small sharp knife to remove the grass in clumps and put directly on to the cake, gently pushing the base of the grass on to the cake with the knife so that it sticks. Make sure you add some grass to the base of the kite string to cover the hole into the cake.

14 To finish off the cake, fit the piping nozzle in the other small piping bag and fill with the rest of the royal icing. Pipe a little icing on the back of each flower and the bases of the toadstools and arrange over the cakes and the board. If using, add the rabbit to the top of the cake and position to look as if he or she is holding the kite string.

Giant Cupcake Sprinkles

This is probably the simplest cake in the book to make and decorate, and large cupcake tins are now readily available and take all of the hard work out of creating an impressive cake. You could create a chocolate version with chocolate buttercream and sprinkles.

FOR THE CAKE

Cake mix for 20cm/8in
   round madeira cake (see
   page 10)
½ quantity buttercream (see
   page 14)
Pink food colouring
Multi-coloured sugar
   sprinkles

EQUIPMENT

Large cupcake tin or pan
Baking parchment
Wire cooling rack
Elbow joint
1.5cm/⅔in star nozzle
Large piping (pastry) bag
Rotating cake turntable
20cm/8in round cake board
   or cake stand
Plastic dowel
Small plastic jar of sugar
   sprinkles
Clear film or plastic wrap
Adhesive tape
Sharp knife
Wide pink ribbon

METHOD

1 Preheat the oven to 160ºC/325ºF/
Gas 3. Grease the cupcake tin
well and cut a circle of baking
parchment to fit the round base
of the bottom section. Divide the
cake mix between the two halves of
the tin and bake for 40–45 minutes.
Once baked leave to cool for
10 minutes in the tins then remove
and leave to cool completely on a
wire cooling rack.

2 When ready to assemble the
cake, colour the buttercream with
the pink food colouring. Spread a
layer of buttercream on to the base
cake and place the top of the cake
on this, pressing down gently.

3 Insert the elbow joint into the
centre of the top of the cake, pushing
it down so the angle of the joint is in
line with the peak of the cake.

9 Then, make a small hole in the clear film for the dowel to fit through.

10 Push the top end of the dowel into the sprinkle pot for it to balance on, and gently tip the sprinkles down to cover the dowel.

11 To finish, tie the pink ribbon around the centre of the bottom half of the cake in a bow.

4 Fit the star nozzle in the piping bag and then fill the bag with the buttercream. Starting from the centre of the cake pipe the buttercream right round the cake in an even line, working up the cake as you go – if you have a cake turntable place the board on this as it will make the piping easier. Finish the piping with a peak at the top.

5 Spread a small amount of buttercream in the centre of the cake board or stand and carefully place the cupcake on top, pushing down gently to stick.

6 Scatter the sugar sprinkles over the cake with a larger pile at the top – you need to do this soon after you have finished piping or the sprinkles won't stick to the buttercream.

7 Push the dowel into the elbow joint and mark the point where it comes out of the top of the joint. Then remove the dowel again and spread buttercream on to the top part above your mark, and cover this buttercream in a thick layer of sprinkles; leave the top 5cm/2in of the dowel uncovered and re-insert into the cake. Stick more sprinkles over the join if necessary.

8 Empty a few sprinkles out of the full pot and cover the top of the pot with clear film. Stick in place with a piece of tape, sealing it firmly to make the film as smooth and invisible as possible.

Creepy-Crawly Halloween

A spooky treat to form the centrepiece for a Halloween party. The spider and web will need making the day before in order to set, and if you can't find any ready-made spiders you can always make some extra smaller ones to decorate the cake with.

FOR THE CAKES

400g/14oz black sugarpaste
Edible glue
100g/3½oz black flower paste
Piece of dried spaghetti
Tiny ball of red flower paste
100g/3½oz black candy melts
Trex or vegetable shortening
20cm/8in round madeira cake (see page 10)
15cm/6in round madeira cake (see page 10)
¼ quantity buttercream (see page 14)
1.5kg/3lb 5oz orange sugarpaste
Black writing icing
4 edible candy spiders

EQUIPMENT

8 blanking caps
25cm/10in round base board
Long foundation rod
Locking nut
Narrow black ribbon
Rolling pin
Chopsticks
Small sharp knife
Small balling tool
No. 3 plain nozzle
2 small piping (pastry) bags
Piece of acetate
Apple corer
Sharp knife
15cm/6in round platform
2 short rods
Rotating angled cake turntable (optional)
Black florist's tape
50cm/20in wire

METHOD

1 Fit 4 of the blanking caps into the outside holes on the base board, leaving the middle hole free. Cover the board with the black sugarpaste (see page 19) and make the hole in the paste for the foundation rod. Attach the rod to the board with the locking nut and leave to set overnight. Using a little edible glue, stick the black ribbon around the edge of the base board.

2 To make the main spider take 25g/1oz of the black flower paste and roll into a small ball for the head. Divide the remaining flower paste and shape one half into an oval, shaping one end to make it thinner than the other then flattening both ends slightly. Brush the ends with a edible glue, then insert one end of the piece of spaghetti into the thicker end of the body, push the other end into the head and stick the two together. Lightly score the back of the body with a small sharp knife to create a hairy back effect.

3 With the last piece of flower paste roll out the 8 spider legs. Stick 3 of the legs to each side of the body and 2 long thin ones to the front. Place a chopstick under each leg to hold them in place while they dry and curl the 2 front legs around the head.

4 With a small balling tool make 2 small indents for the eyes. Roll 2 pieces of red flower paste into tiny balls and stick the eyes in place with a little edible glue.

Tumbling Macarons

Macarons are pretty and sophisticated, and this tumbling display will make everyone smile. Beautiful yet simple to create using ready-made pastries, the colours of the icing, ribbon and gift box can be easily changed to reflect your chosen macarons.

FOR THE CAKE

1.4kg/3lb 1½oz pale lime-
    green sugarpaste
Edible glue
20cm/8in round madeira
    cake (see page 10)
¼ quantity buttercream (see
    page 14)
20–24 macarons
25g/1oz royal icing

EQUIPMENT

4 blanking caps
25cm/10in round base
    board
Long foundation rod
Locking nut
Narrow pink ribbon
Apple corer
Sharp knife
Elbow joint
Long rod
Round card gift box or pot
Wide pink organza ribbon

METHOD

1 Fit the blanking caps into the 4 outer holes of the base board. Cover the board with 400g/14oz of the pale lime-green sugarpaste (see page 19) and make a hole in the centre of the board for the foundation rod. Attach the rod to the board with the locking nut and leave to set overnight. Using a little glue stick the narrow pink ribbon around the edge of the board.

2 When ready to assemble, make a hole in the centre of the cake using an apple corer for the rod to fit through, ensuring the hole goes right through the cake and rubbing the inside of the hole lightly with your finger to remove excess crumbs.

3 Cover the cake with buttercream and the remaining pale lime-green sugarpaste (see page 19). Using the tip of a sharp knife make a small incision in the icing into the hole in the cake, then gently lift the cake on to the board, pushing the rod through the hole.

4 Smooth the sides of the cake again, pushing the icing down to meet the icing on the board. Insert the elbow joint into the foundation rod and then attach the long rod to that.

5 Working from the cake upwards, stick macarons to the rod using a little royal icing for each one. Hold the macarons in place for a few seconds to make sure they stick securely.

6 Once the icing has set, balance the box on top of the macarons and arrange the remaining macarons around the top of the cake, sticking in place with royal icing. Tie the ribbon around the cake finishing with a bow at the front.

Pot of Paint

Show off your sugarcrafting skills with this impressive paint pot cake. Candy melts come in a great variety of colours so the paint colour can be easily adapted to suit every DIY enthusiast. The brush needs making at least 24 hours in advance in order to set.

FOR THE CAKE

400g/14oz white sugarpaste
Edible glue
100g/3½oz navy flower
    paste
50g/2oz light brown flower
    paste
500g/1lb 2oz grey
    sugarpaste
2 x 13cm/5in round madeira
    cakes (see page 10)
¼ quantity buttercream (see
    page 14)
50g/2oz pink sugarpaste
150g/5oz red candy melts

EQUIPMENT

4 blanking caps
25cm/10in round base
    board
Long foundation rod
Locking nut
Narrow white ribbon
Rolling pin
Small sharp knife
Ruler
45cm/18in wire
Apple corer
11cm/4¼in round cutter
5cm/2in round cutter
Small star cutter
22-gauge wire
1cm/½in round cutter
5mm/¼in round cutter

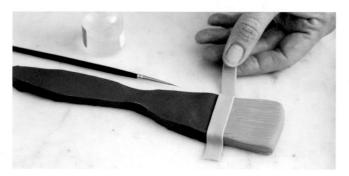

METHOD

1 Fit the blanking caps into the 4 outer holes of the base board. Cover the board with the white sugarpaste (see page 19) and make a hole in the centre of the board for the foundation rod. Attach the rod to the board with the locking nut and leave to set overnight. Using a little edible glue stick the narrow white ribbon around the edge of the board.

2 To make the paintbrush, roll out the navy flower paste thickly and cut out the handle shape using the template on page 126, with a small sharp knife.

3 Roll out the light brown flower paste to a small rectangle the same thickness as the handle, making one end the same width as the handle and the other end very

slightly wider. Round the edges of the wider end slightly then using a small sharp knife score down the length to create the brush bristles. Use a little glue to stick the two pieces together.

4 Take a small ball of grey sugarpaste and roll out, then cut a long strip 1.5cm/⅔in x 10cm/4in. Brush the back of the strip with glue and wrap around the paintbrush, covering the join. Roll two small balls of grey and stick to the strip with glue to create rivets.

5 Gently push the piece of wire into the paintbrush, making sure it goes in as close to the end as possible so that the wire supports the whole brush. Leave to dry for at least 24 hours.

Art Gallery Paint Splats

Let the abstract artist inside you run riot on this dramatic cake, with explosions of paint in all directions. The paint splatters are fun and easy to create. The paint tubes will need to be made the day before to enable them to set fully.

FOR THE CAKES

1.9kg/4lb 4oz black
 sugarpaste
150g/5oz grey flower paste
50g/2oz yellow flower paste
Edible glue
50g/2oz red flower paste
15cm/6in round madeira
 cake (see page 10)
20cm/8in round madeira
 cake (see page 10)
¼ quantity buttercream (see
 page 14)
100g/3½oz lime green
 candy melts
100g/3½oz red candy melts
100g/3½oz yellow candy
 melts

EQUIPMENT

8 blanking caps
25cm/10in round base
 board
Long foundation rod
Locking nut
Rolling pin
Small sharp knife
2 wooden dowels, 1 cut to
 20cm/8in and 1 cut
 to 25cm/10in
Apple corer
2.5cm/1in short rod
2 x 5cm/2in medium rods
Collar
3 small piping (pastry) bags
15cm/6in round cake
 platform
22-gauge wire
Narrow black ribbon

METHOD

1 Fit 4 of the blanking caps into the centre and 3 of the outer holes of the base board. Cover the board with 400g/14oz of the black sugarpaste (see page 19) and make a hole for the long foundation rod. Attach the rod to the board with the locking nut and leave to set overnight.

2 Take half of the grey flower paste and roll into a paint tube shape. Flatten the shape slightly and pinch the fatter end to flatten completely. Cut the top section off the paint tube shape.

3 Take the yellow flower paste and shape to match the centre section of the tube. Apply a little edible glue to each end of the yellow piece of flower paste and then stick the two grey ends of the tube either side. Gently push the three pieces together and smooth the edges. Gently push the shorter wooden dowel into the paint tube.

4 Roll out a piece of the remaining grey flower paste and cut a small strip 5mm/¼in wide. Brush a little glue around the join of the dowel and paint tube then stick the strip around. Trim to fit with a small sharp knife, then use the back of the knife to create lines on this strip to look like the screw threads for the cap.

5 Repeat the above with most of the remaining grey flower paste and the red flower paste to create the red paint tube. Gently push the longer wooden dowel into the red paint tube. Leave both the tubes to dry for at least 24 hours.

6 When ready to assemble, make a hole in the centre of the smaller cake from the bottom with an apple corer. Ensure the hole goes only to the centre of the cake – you don't want it to go right through. Make a hole to one side of the larger cake with the apple corer, this time making sure the hole goes right through the cake. Rub both holes lightly with your finger to remove excess crumbs.

7 Cover the larger cake with two-thirds of the buttercream and 1kg/ 2¼lb of the black sugarpaste (see page 19). Then, cover the smaller cake with buttercream and the remaining black sugarpaste. Make a small incision in the top of the larger cake through the icing into the hole.

Pick 'N' Mix Extravaganza

This colourful bonanza is a great combination of brightly layered sponge on a classic madeira base. Choosing candies to decorate with is almost as much fun as making the cake itself. This is a project that can be made and assembled in a day.

FOR THE CAKES

400g/14oz pale pink
sugarpaste

Cake mix for 20cm/8in
madeira cake (see page
10) but leave out the plain
(all-purpose) flour

23cm/9in round madeira
cake (see page 10)

Pink, orange, yellow, green
and purple food colouring

½ quantity buttercream (see
page 14)

1.75kg/3lb 14oz white
sugarpaste

50g/2oz white candy melts

Large jelly hearts

Edible glue

Mixture of sweets or
candies

EQUIPMENT

4 blanking caps

25cm/10in round base
board

Long foundation rod

Locking nut

5 x 18cm/5in sandwich tins
or pans

Skewer

Wire cooling racks

Apple corer

Pale pink ribbon

Sharp knife

3 long rods

Medium rod

Elbow joint

Decorative card gift box

METHOD

1 Fit 4 of the blanking caps into 3 of the outside holes and the centre hole on the base board. Cover the board with the pale pink sugarpaste (see page 19) and make a hole in the paste for the foundation rod. Attach the rod to the board with the locking nut and leave to set overnight.

2 Preheat the oven to 180ºC/350ºF/Gas 4 and make up the cake mix, remembering to omit the plain flour. Divide the mix evenly between 5 bowls, and add a little of each of the food colourings to the bowls, beating well between each addition so that you get an even colour. Fill each of the sandwich tins with a different coloured cake mix, smooth the tops and then bake for 25–30

minutes until firm to the touch and a skewer inserted into the centre comes out clean. Turn the cakes out on to wire cooling racks and leave to cool completely.

3 When ready to assemble, spread a layer of buttercream on the top of one cake and top with another. Repeat with the rest of the layers, spreading buttercream in between.

4 Make a hole towards the back of both the 23cm/9in cake and the layered cake with an apple corer, for the rods to fit through. Ensure the hole goes right through both cakes, and rub the holes lightly with your finger to remove excess crumbs.

Piggy Bank

Using a polystyrene ball ensures you get a smooth and round shape which is easy to wrap in sugarpaste. The piggy bank is best made the day before, but the tablecloth needs to be made on the day of assembly to ensure it is soft enough to drape over the cake.

FOR THE CAKE

250g/9oz blue sugarpaste

Edible glue

Tiny amount of black
  sugarpaste

1.75kg/3lb 14oz white
  sugarpaste

20cm/8in square madeira
  cake (see page 10)

¼ quantity buttercream (see
  page 14)

Trex or vegetable
  shortening

250g/9oz red sugarpaste

50g/2oz brown candy melts

3 bags of chocolate coins

EQUIPMENT

Rolling pin

Ruler

10cm/4in round polystyrene
  or Styrofoam ball

Small sharp knife

Small balling tool

2cm/¾in triangle cutter

4 blanking caps

30cm/12in square base
  board

Long foundation rod

Locking nut

Short rod

Narrow blue ribbon

Apple corer

Piece of acetate

4cm/1½in square cutter

Cake smoothers

2cm/¾in round cutter

Palette knife

Long rod

30cm/12in wooden dowel

METHOD

1 To make the piggy bank, roll out the blue sugarpaste to a 30cm/12in circle. Lightly brush the polystyrene ball with a little cooled, boiled water then place it in the centre of the sugarpaste circle. Bring the edges of the sugarpaste around the ball to enclose completely, trim off the excess and seal the edges. Lightly roll the ball on the work surface to smooth the surface.

2 Using the trimmings of the blue sugarpaste, shape a piece into a large, round, thick disk for the nose. Using the balling tool make 2 small indents in the nose for the nostrils. Roll more sugarpaste into a thick sausage shape and cut 4 smaller round discs for the feet. Roll out the remaining sugarpaste and cut out 2 triangles for the ears.

3 With a little edible glue attach the 4 feet to the base of the ball and the nose to the front. Stick the ears in place with a little more glue. Roll the black sugarpaste into 2 tiny balls for the eyes and stick those either side of the nose with the edible glue. Leave to dry overnight.

4 Fit the blanking caps into the 4 outer holes of the base board. Cover the board with 400g/14oz of the white sugarpaste (see page 19) and make a hole in the centre of the paste for the foundation rod.

5 Attach the rod to the board with the locking nut, add the short rod and leave to set overnight. Using a little edible glue stick the narrow blue ribbon around the edge of the board.

6 When ready to assemble, make a hole in the centre of the cake using an apple corer for the rod to fit through, ensuring the hole goes right through the cake, and rub the inside of the hole lightly with your finger to remove excess crumbs.

7 Cover the cake in the butter-cream and 1kg/2¼lb of the white sugarpaste (see page 19). Then gently lift the cake on to the board,

pushing the rod through the hole. Smooth the sides of the cake again pushing the icing down to meet the icing on the board.

8 Spread a thin layer of trex on the sheet of acetate. Roll out the remaining white sugarpaste and cut out 13 x 4cm/1½in squares. Roll out the red sugarpaste and cut 12 squares using the same cutter. Lightly brush the edges of each of the squares with edible glue and, alternating colours, stick the squares together to create the tablecloth on the piece of acetate.

9 Once you have stuck all the squares together lightly roll with a rolling pin to create a smooth surface, and push the outer edges in with cake smoothers to make sure that the small squares are stuck together securely. Cut a 2cm/¾in round hole in the middle of the tablecloth to fit over the rod and leave to dry for 30 minutes.

10 Loosen the tablecloth from the acetate with a palette knife then gently lift on to the cake over the foundation rod at an angle and

smooth on to the cake, draping the corners over the edges. Insert the long rod into the short rod.

11 Make a money slot in the top of the piggy bank with a small sharp knife, then push the wooden dowel into the slot. Put the other end of the wooden dowel into the long rod so the piggy bank sits upside down above the cake.

12 In a small bowl melt the brown candy melts, either in the microwave on a medium heat, or over a pan of gently simmering water; be careful not to overheat or they will become grainy.

13 Using a small palette knife coat the rods and wooden dowel with the candy melts. Starting at the bottom stick the chocolate coins on to the rods by adding a little extra of the melted candy melts to each one and holding it in place for a few seconds to make sure that they stick firmly.

14 Ensure that the entire rod is covered and if need be, add coins on top of the first layer, to create a tumbling effect. Pile the remaining chocolate coins on top of the cake, and leave to set for at least an hour before serving.

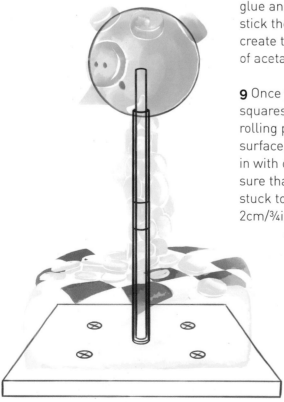

Piping Bag Trompe L'Oeil

A chance to show off both your piping and sugarcrafting skills, the decorations on the cake can be easily changed and could even include some writing if you wanted to personalise the cake with a message. The piping bag will need making the day before.

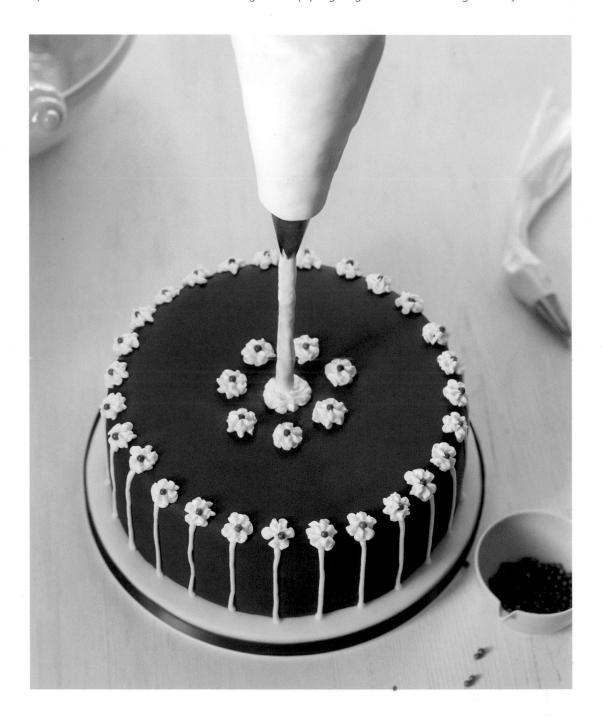

FOR THE CAKE

400g/14oz white sugarpaste
Edible glue
250g/9oz white flower paste
20cm/8in round madeira
    cake (see page 10)
¼ quantity buttercream (see
    page 14)
1kg/2¼lb fuchsia pink
    sugarpaste
100g/3½oz royal icing
Purple sugar pearls

EQUIPMENT

4 blanking caps
25cm/10in round base
    board
Short foundation rod
Locking nut
5cm/2in medium rod
Narrow fuchsia pink ribbon
14cm/5½in polystyrene or
    Styrofoam cone
Hacksaw or large serrated
    knife
Soft brush
Metal skewer
Rolling pin
Ruler
Sharp knife
Large star nozzle
Wooden dowel
Apple corer
Rotating angled cake
    turntable (optional)
No. 2 plain nozzle
2 small piping (pastry) bags
Small star nozzle

METHOD

1 Fit the blanking caps into the 4 outer holes of the base board. Cover the board with the white sugarpaste (see page 19) and make a hole in the centre for the foundation rod. Attach the rod to the board with the locking nut, then add the medium

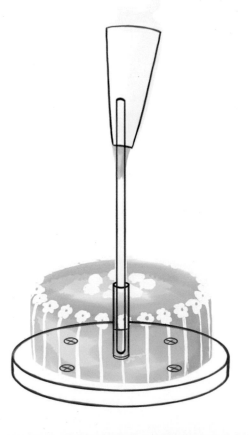

rod and leave to set overnight. Using a little glue stick the narrow fuchsia pink ribbon around the edge of the board.

2 To make the piping bag roll, take the polystyrene cone and cut about 5cm/2in from the wider end with a hacksaw, or large serrated knife. Brush the end with a soft brush to remove any loose bits. Push a metal skewer into the tip of the cone down its length to make a hole for the dowel to go into.

3 Roll out the white flower paste to a rectangle 16cm/6¼in x 20cm/8in. Brush the cone with a little cooled boiled water and shake off any excess. Place the tip of the cone against one short edge of the flower paste and wrap it around the cone.

Bucket of Popcorn

A bright bucket overflowing with popcorn offers two treats in one cake. If you can't find a sweet scoop you could always have the popcorn tumbling from a bag or box, and with no sugarpaste decorations this cake can be made and assembled in a day.

FOR THE CAKE

400g/14oz blue sugarpaste
Edible glue
15cm/6in round madeira
cake (see page 10)
12.5cm/5in round madeira
cake (see page 10)
¼ quantity buttercream (see
page 14)
900g/2lb white sugarpaste
200g/7oz red sugarpaste
50g/2oz white candy melts
150g/5oz bag of toffee
popcorn

EQUIPMENT

4 blanking caps
25cm/10in round base
board
Long foundation rod
Locking nut
Medium rod
Narrow red ribbon
Large serrated knife
Pastry brush
Apple corer
Rolling pin
Ruler
Elbow joint
Connector
Cake smoother
Wooden dowel
Plastic scoop
Adhesive tape

METHOD

1 Fit the blanking caps into the 4 outer holes of the base board. Cover the board with the blue sugarpaste (see page 19) and make a hole in the middle for the long foundation rod. Attach the rod to the board with the locking nut, insert the medium rod into the foundation rod and leave to set overnight. Using a little glue stick the narrow red ribbon around the edge of the board.

2 When ready to assemble, place the larger cake on top of the smaller one, then with a large serrated knife trim the sides of both cakes to form a bucket shape. Make a hole in the centre with an apple corer, making sure the hole goes right through both cakes. Brush away any excess crumbs with a pastry brush.

3 Sandwich the cakes together with a little of the buttercream and then cover the top and sides of the cakes with the remaining buttercream. Take 100g/3½oz of the white

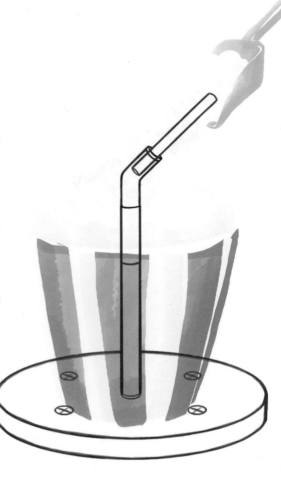

sugarpaste and roll out a 6cm/2½in circle for the top of the cake. Cut a 2cm/¾in hole out of the centre, then put it in place over the rods and smooth down.

4 Cover the sides of the cake with 700g/1lb 8oz of the white sugarpaste (see page 19). Fold the top edge of the icing over the top of the cake so that it covers the edge of the sugarpaste circle.

5 Gently lift the cake on to the covered board over the rods and smooth the sides of the cake to ensure the icing neatly meets the icing on the board. Add the elbow joint and connector to the medium rod.

Magical Writing Quill

A mysterious letter being written by an invisible hand, this antique-looking cake is easy to cut and serve for a crowd. The parchment and inkpot will need making the day before. Write a personal message in black icing on the parchment for a special recipient.

FOR THE CAKE

150g/5oz ivory flower paste
50g/2oz black sugarpaste
1.5kg/3lb 5oz brown
  sugarpaste
600g/1lb 6oz ivory
  sugarpaste
Edible glue
25cm/10in square madeira
  cake (see page 10)
¼ quantity buttercream (see
  page 14)
Dark brown gel food
  colouring
Black sugar art pen

EQUIPMENT

Rolling pin
Sharp knife
Long ruler
Chopsticks
Icing smoothers
3cm/1⅛in round cutter
2.5cm/1in round cutter
35cm/14in square cake
  board, with all 5 blanking
  caps in place, or just a
  cake board
Narrow brown ribbon
Fine paintbrush
Black florist's tape
25cm/10in wire
Fake feather quill

METHOD

1 To make the parchment paper, roll out the ivory flower paste thinly and cut out a 15cm/6in x 22cm/8⅔in rectangle. Curl the top two corners slightly and roll up the bottom edge loosely using chopsticks to support the paste.

2 Take the black sugarpaste and shape into a square for the inkpot. Take a small ball of the brown sugarpaste and roll into a thick disc and cut out a 3cm/1⅛in circle. Stick the brown disc on to the black square with a little glue, then push the 2.5cm/1in cutter into the circle to create an indent for the lid.

3 Cover the board with the ivory sugarpaste (see page 19). Using a little edible glue stick the narrow brown ribbon around the edge of the board. Leave the parchment, ink pot and cake board to dry overnight.

4 When ready to assemble, cover the cake with the buttercream and the remaining brown sugarpaste (see page 19). Gently lift the cake on to the covered cake board and smooth down the edges of the cake to ensure the icing neatly meets the icing on the board.

Shooting Star Rocket

A rocket firework shooting out of this cake could look even more dramatic with the addition of indoor sparklers. The rocket will need making and assembling the day before in order to set before adding to the cake.

FOR THE CAKE

1kg/2¼lb navy sugarpaste
750g/1lb 10oz black
   sugarpaste
Edible glue
250g/9oz yellow sugarpaste
50g/2oz red sugarpaste
50g/2oz orange sugarpaste
20cm/8in square madeira
   cake (see page 10)
¼ quantity buttercream (see
   page 14)
15ml/1 tbsp royal icing

EQUIPMENT

4 blanking caps
30cm/12in square base
   board
Short foundation rod
Locking nut
Narrow yellow ribbon
Rolling pin
Ruler
4cm/1½in round cutter
14cm/5½in cardboard tube
9cm/3½in round cutter
Star cutters – small,
   medium and large
22-gauge silver wire
Apple corer
Elbow joint
Wooden dowel
Yellow straw

METHOD

1 Set aside 50g/2oz of the navy sugarpaste then mix together the rest with the black sugarpaste, kneading thoroughly to ensure the colours are evenly mixed. Fit the blanking caps into the 4 outer holes of the base board.

2 Cover the board with 500g/1¼lb of the mixed navy and black sugarpaste (see page 19) and make a hole in the centre of the board for the foundation rod. Attach the rod to the board with the locking nut and leave to set overnight. Using a little edible glue stick the narrow yellow ribbon around the edge of the board.

3 To make the rocket, roll out the yellow sugarpaste and cut out a 14cm/5½in square and a 4cm/1½in circle. Brush the cardboard tube with edible glue then wrap the yellow square around the outside, pushing the edges together to seal. Gently roll the tube to ensure the sugarpaste is smooth.

4 Cut a small hole in the centre of the yellow circle for the dowel to fit through then brush the edge with a little glue and stick the circle to the base of the rocket.

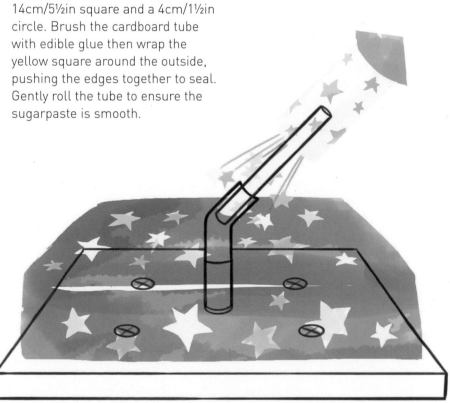

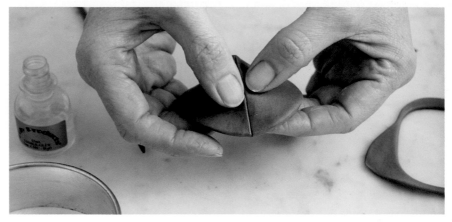

5 Roll out the reserved navy sugarpaste and cut a 9cm/3½in circle and stars in various sizes. Cut a wedge out of the circle then shape the circle round to form a cone, overlap the edges a little and stick with glue, pressing together gently to seal. Standing the yellow rocket upright, stick the navy cone to the top end with more glue, and then stick the navy stars around the sides.

6 Roll out the remaining yellow sugarpaste and cut out stars in various sizes. Insert wire into some of the stars to use as shooting sparks, and secure in place with a little edible glue. Repeat the above with the red and orange sugarpaste, ensuring you have a mix of stars in all colours and sizes. Leave the rocket and stars to dry for at least 24 hours.

7 When you are ready to assemble make a hole in the centre of the cake using an apple corer for the rod to fit through, ensuring the hole goes right through the cake and rubbing the inside of the hole lightly with your finger to remove excess crumbs.

8 Spread the buttercream over the cake and cover the cake with the remaining mixed navy and black sugarpaste (see page 19). Using the tip of a sharp knife make a small incision in the centre of the cake through the icing, then gently lift the cake on to the board, pushing the rod through the hole. Smooth the sides of the cake, again pushing the icing down to meet the icing on the board. Insert the elbow joint into the foundation rod.

9 Brush a little of the royal icing in the hole in the bottom of the rocket then insert the wooden dowel into the hole, adding a little more royal icing to ensure the dowel sticks in place.

10 Slide a yellow straw over the dowel then push the end of the dowel into the elbow joint.

11 Spread some royal icing over the end of the angle joint that is showing, and the base of the straw, then stick some of the yellow stars

to the icing, holding them in place for a few seconds so that they stick, and making sure that the elbow joint is completely covered.

12 Take the stars on wires and cut the wire to various lengths and then gently push them into the bottom of the rocket at different angles to create the shooting stars. Finally, stick the loose yellow, red and orange stars to the top and sides of the cake, again mixing up the sizes and colours as you go.

Rose Petal Cascade

This beautiful tiered rose petal cake would make an ideal informal wedding cake and extra tiers could be added if need be. The petals are easy to make in advance and once they cascade from the confetti box they create a stunning display.

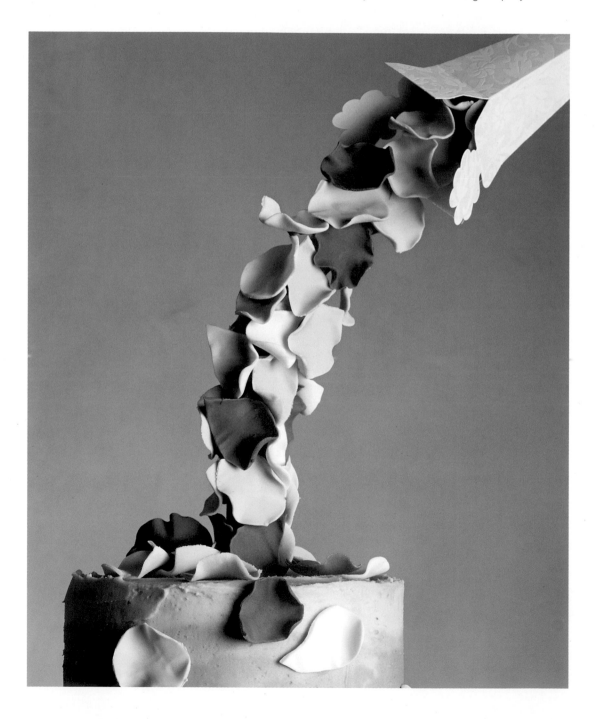

FOR THE CAKE

50g/2oz fuchsia pink flower paste

50g/2oz pale pink flower paste

50g/2oz baby pale pink flower paste

20cm/8in round madeira cake (see page 10)

15cm/6in round madeira cake (see page 10)

1 quantity buttercream (see page 14)

Pink food colouring

EQUIPMENT

Non-stick board

Rolling pin

Rose petal cutters, medium and small

Foam pad

Balling tool

Flower shapers or teaspoons

Apple corer

30cm/12in cake stand or board

Small palette knife

Icing scraper

2 long rods

15cm/6in cake platform

Elbow joint

Wooden dowel

Confetti box

METHOD

1 To make the rose petals roll out the fuchsia pink flower paste on a non-stick board to a very thin round. Cut out petals in both sizes. Place on a foam pad and, using the balling tool, shape and thin the edges of the petals to create a frilled edge. Leave each one to dry in a flower shaper, or over the back of a teaspoon.

2 Repeat the above with the pale pink and baby pale pink flower pastes and leave all of the petals for at least 24 hours to dry completely.

3 When ready to assemble, make a hole in the centre of both the 20cm/8in and 15cm/6in cakes with an apple corer for the rods to fit through. Ensure the hole goes right through both cakes, rubbing the holes lightly with your finger to remove excess crumbs.

4 Cover the top and sides of each cake with a thin layer of buttercream, then leave to chill in the refrigerator for half an hour.

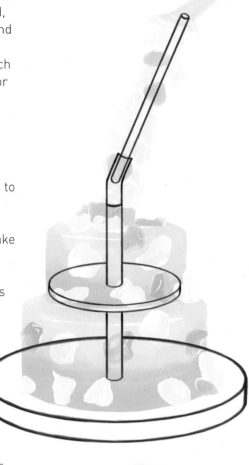

Santa and Sleigh

A perfect Christmas cake for the kids as an alternative to the traditional fruit cake.
The soaring reindeer, jolly Santa figure and sleigh will all need making the day before to
ensure they are fully set before assembling.

FOR THE CAKE

Edible glue
250g/9oz brown flower
  paste
250g/9oz red flower paste
25g/1oz white flower paste
15g/½oz black flower paste
Tiny amount of yellow
  flower paste
25g/1oz flesh-coloured
  flower paste
Piece of dried spaghetti
1 quantity royal icing
600g/1lb 6oz white
  sugarpaste
20cm/8in square madeira
  cake (see page 10)
¼ quantity buttercream (see
  page 14)
1.5kg/3lb 5oz brown
  sugarpaste
Yellow food colouring
Icing (confectioners') sugar,
  for dusting

EQUIPMENT

2 x 60cm/24in lengths of wire
Black florist's tape
Rolling pin
Sharp knife
Reindeer cutter (or use the
  template on p127)
Dresden tool
Small balling tool
Small round cutter
3 blanking caps
35cm/14in square cake board
2 short foundation rods
2 locking nuts
Large serrated knife
Apple corer
Long ruler
2 elbow joints
Narrow red ribbon
Piping (pastry) bag
No. 2 writing nozzle
Small palette knife

METHOD

1 To make the reindeer, first cover both lengths of wire in the black florist's tape, securing each end with a little edible glue. Roll out the brown flower paste and cut out 12 reindeer shapes, then leave to dry for about 30 minutes to firm up slightly.

2 Meanwhile roll out 125g/4¼oz of the red flower paste and cut out 2 sleigh pieces (see template page 126). Set aside to dry overnight.

3 Next make the Santa Claus. Take a third of the remaining red sugarpaste and roll into a small ball for Santa's body, then shape this into a cone, keeping the bottom half round for his tummy. Roll 2 sausages for his legs, squeeze one end to flatten and use a little glue to stick these flattened ends to the sides of his body.

4 Make 2 slightly shorter, thinner sausages for his arms and again squeeze the ends to flatten. Roll out a little of the white flower paste and cut 2 thin strips to use for the cuffs, stick these to the fat ends of Santa's arms a little in from the ends then stick the arms to either side of his body, squeezing them gently to make sure they stick.

5 Cut another slightly wider strip from the white flower paste for the front of Santa's coat and stick this to the centre of his body. Roll 2 small balls of white flower paste for his hands and stick these to the ends of his arms then with the Dresden tool make small indents to create his thumbs.

6 Take a little of the black flower paste and roll 2 small balls for his boots, flatten each end and then stick to the legs.

7 Roll out some more of the black flower paste and cut a strip for his belt. Stick this around his tummy and add a small square of yellow flower paste for the buckle.

8 Shape the flesh-coloured flower paste into a ball for his head, saving a small piece for his nose.

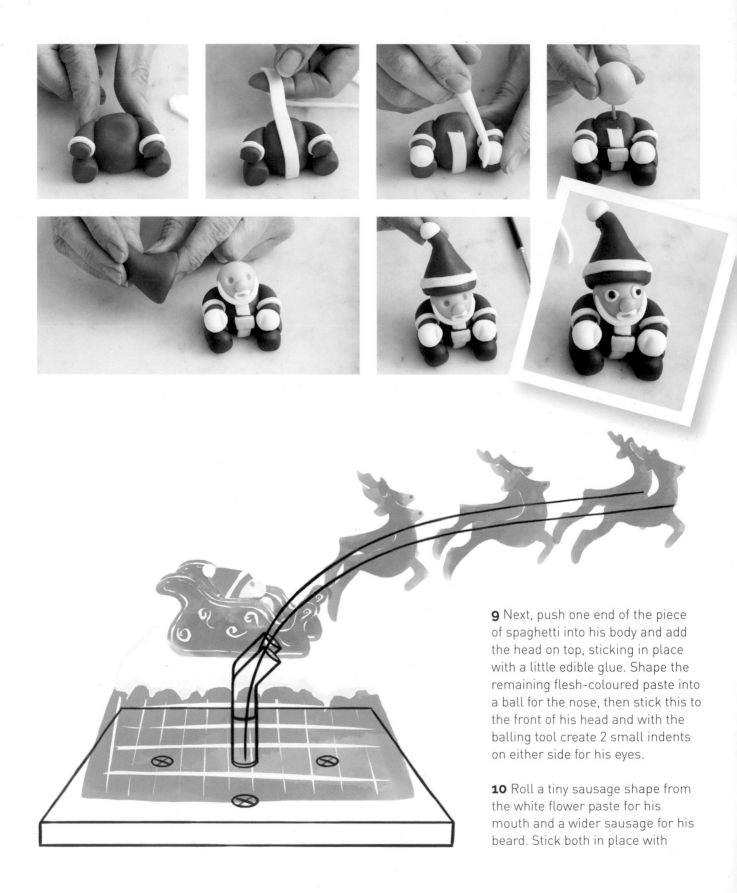

9 Next, push one end of the piece of spaghetti into his body and add the head on top, sticking in place with a little edible glue. Shape the remaining flesh-coloured paste into a ball for the nose, then stick this to the front of his head and with the balling tool create 2 small indents on either side for his eyes.

10 Roll a tiny sausage shape from the white flower paste for his mouth and a wider sausage for his beard. Stick both in place with edible glue. Take the remaining red flower paste – reserving a small ball for the reindeer noses – and shape into a cone for the Santa hat. Make an indent in the thicker end to fit over his head.

11 Add a strip of white flower paste around the base of the hat and a small ball to the end, then, with more edible glue stick the hat on to Santa's head. Cut 2 small white circles for his eyes and 2 even smaller circles of black for the pupils. Stick all of these in place and then leave to dry overnight.

12 To finish the reindeer, lay 3 reindeer down, in a line, on the work surface and spread each one with a little royal icing. Lay one piece of covered wire on top making sure the wire goes over each reindeer at the same point and that they are evenly spaced.

13 Add a little more royal icing on top of the wire and stick 3 more reindeer on top, matching up the edges as best you can. Repeat with the other piece of wire and 6 reindeer. Roll tiny balls of red flower paste for the noses and even smaller balls of black for the eyes

and stick in place with a dab of edible glue. Leave to dry overnight.

14 Fit 3 blanking caps to the cake board, leaving the middle one and front centre one free. Cover the board with the white sugarpaste (see page 19), make 2 holes in the sugarpaste over the unfilled holes and attach a short foundation rod to each, securing with locking nuts. Leave to set overnight.

15 When ready to assemble, first shape the cake into a roof shape with a large serrated knife, then with the apple corer make 2 holes in the cake to correspond with the rod positioning on the cake board, going all the way down. Using the tip of a sharp knife make a small incision through the icing into the holes in the cake.

16 Cover the cake with the buttercream and the brown sugarpaste (see page 19). Gently lift the cake on to the covered cake board and smooth down the edges of the cake to ensure the icing neatly meets the icing on the board.

17 Using the edge of a long ruler push indents into the sides and the top of the cake about 1.5cm/⅔in apart for the roof tiles. With a small sharp knife mark the individual tiles between these lines in a brick-like pattern.

18 Insert the 2 elbow joints into each of the short foundation rods, at an angle facing downwards. Using a little glue stick the narrow red ribbon around the edge of the board.

19 Take a tablespoon of the royal icing and mix in a little yellow food colouring, then add to the piping bag fitted with the No. 2 writing nozzle and pipe decorations on to the sides of the sleigh. With a small palette knife spread the rest of the royal icing on top of the cake, gently pushing it down the sides to create icicles.

20 Lightly dust the top and sides of the cake with icing sugar.

21 Stick the 2 sides of the sleigh in place on either side of the elbow joints and insert the reindeer wires into each one.

22 Create a seat for Santa from a piece of red flower paste, shape it into a small square that fits between the sleigh sides and so that you can see Santa from the side. Stick Santa on to the seat with a little dab of royal icing, then finally roll a small length of black florist's tape to create the ends of the reins and loop this around the wires with the ends finishing in Santa's hands. Leave to set for 1 hour before serving.

Templates

Draw your own templates using the measurements as a guide. Otherwise you can enlarge the templates on a photocopier, or trace the design and draw a grid of evenly spaced squares over your tracing. Draw a larger grid on to another piece of paper and copy the outline square by square. Draw over the lines to make sure they are continuous.

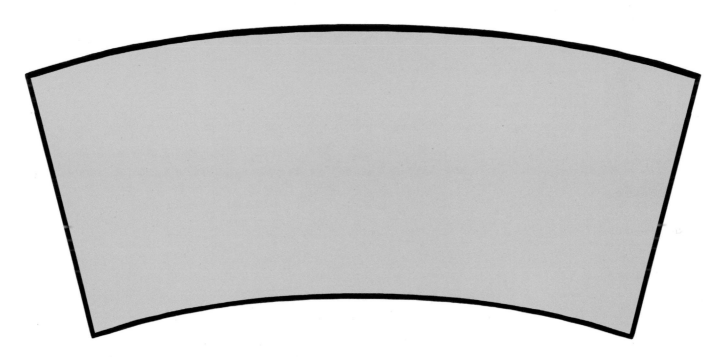

CHRISTMAS PUDDING P50–53
20cm/8in (point to point top edge) x
16cm/6¼in (point to point bottom edge) x
8cm/3⅛in – height at middle point

BUCKET OF POPCORN P102–105
**16cm/6¼in x 4cm/1½in at top and
2.5cm/1in at bottom**

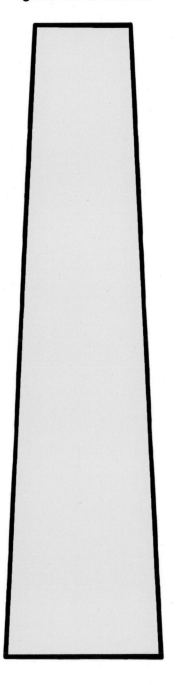

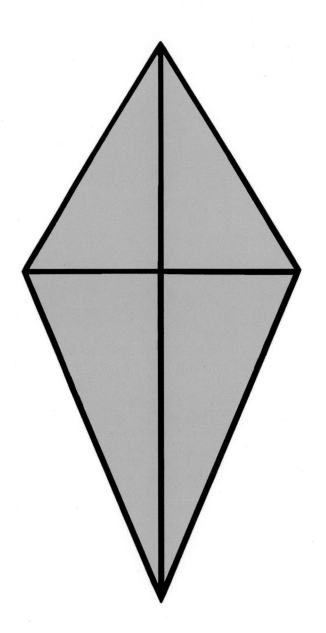

FLYING A KITE P66–69
15cm/6in x 7.5cm/3in

POT OF PAINT P82–85
16cm/6¼in x 5cm/2in – end of brush

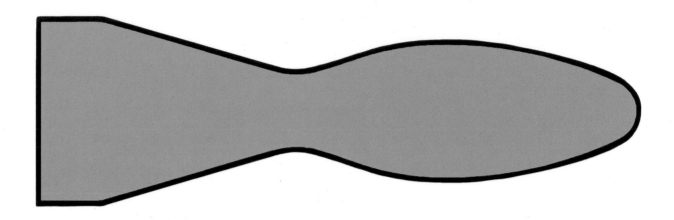

SANTA AND SLEIGH P118–123
**11cm/4¼in along bottom 8cm/3⅛in high
(highest point at the back)**

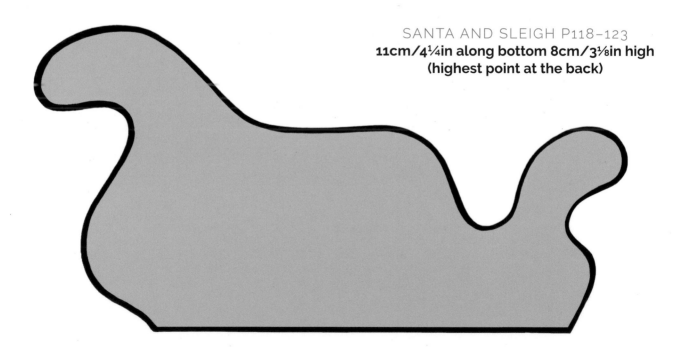

SANTA AND SLEIGH P118–123
11cm/4¼in wide

MAGICAL WRITING QUILL P106–109
5cm/2in x 3.5cm/1⅔in

This edition is published by Lorenz Books
an imprint of Anness Publishing Ltd
info@anness.com
www.annesspublishing.com

© Anness Publishing Ltd 2024

A CIP catalogue record for this book is available from the British Library.

Publisher: Joanna Lorenz
Photography: Nicki Dowey
Food styling: Jayne Cross
Illustrations: Georgie Fearns
Designer: Adelle Mahoney
Editorial: Sarah Lumby
Production Controller: Ben Worley

COOK'S NOTES
Bracketed terms are intended for American readers.
For all recipes, quantities are given in both metric and imperial measures and, where appropriate,
in standard cups and spoons. Follow one set of measures, but not a mixture, because they are not interchangeable.
Standard spoon and cup measures are level. 1 tsp = 5ml, 1 tbsp = 15ml, 1 cup = 250ml/8fl oz.
Australian standard tablespoons are 20ml. Australian readers should use 3 tsp in place of 1 tbsp for measuring small quantities.
American pints are 16fl oz/2 cups. American readers should use 20fl oz/2.5 cups in place of 1 pint when measuring liquids.
Medium (US large) eggs are used unless otherwise stated.

PUBLISHER'S NOTE
Although the advice and information in this book are believed to be accurate at the time of going to press,
neither the author nor the publisher can accept any legal responsibility or liability for any errors or omissions
that may have been made nor for any inaccuracies nor for any loss, harm or injury that comes about
from following instructions or advice in this book.

PICTURE CREDITS
p13 bl Shutterstock/Ana Photo

There is now a wide range of shapes and sizes of kit available but for most of the cakes
within this book I would recommend a Cake Frame starter kit – available from many online retail outlets.
An Anti-gravity Pouring Cake Kit could also be used for many of the designs in this book and again are available online.

ABOUT THE AUTHOR

Jayne Cross has been a "foodie" all her life and a professional food
stylist and writer for more than 20 years. After an earlier successful career
as a high street fashion buyer, she made a bold decision to change direction
completely and pursue her love of all things culinary. At that point she went back
to college to study a City and Guilds Diploma in Professional Cookery before
working on the restaurant frontline as a chef, and then moving into the publishing
world as a food stylist and writer. Since then she has completed a NCFE cake
decorating and sugarcraft course, started her own cake business and worked
on innumerable magazines, advertisements, television shows and over 30
books, specializing in cakes and cake decorating. She is also a lecturer
in Food Styling at the renowned Leiths School of Food and Wine.

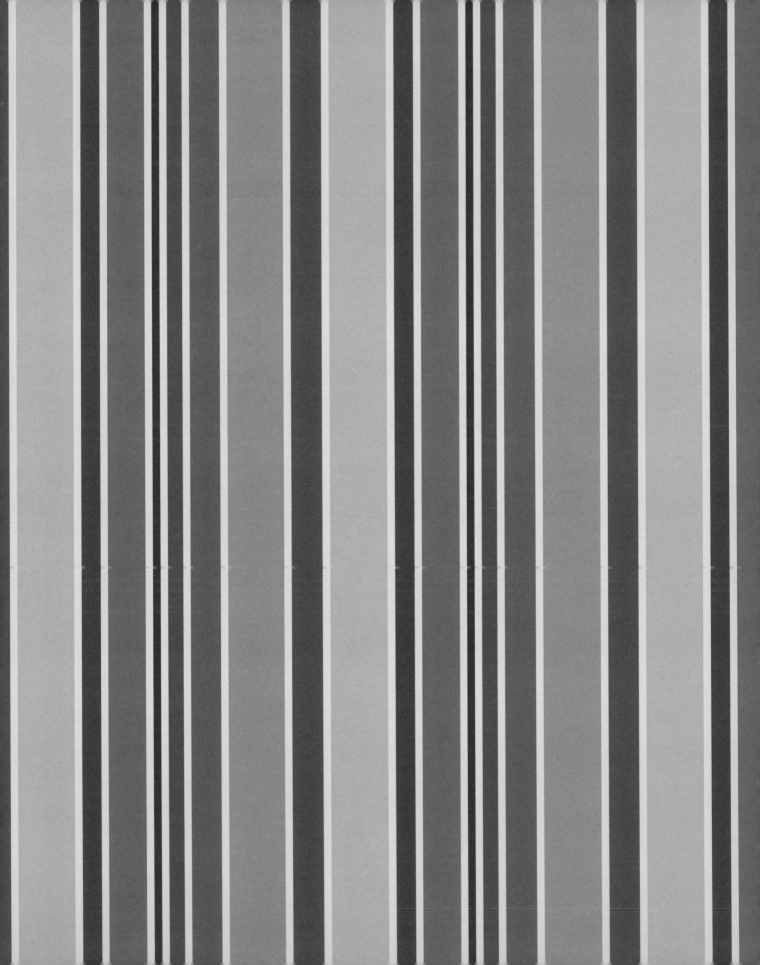